MOUNTAIN
BEARS

TEXT AND PHOTOGRAPHS BY

Wayne Lynch

FIFTH
HOUSE
PUBLISHERS

Front and back cover images by Wayne Lynch
Cover and interior design by John Luckhurst / GDL

The publisher gratefully acknowledges the support of
The Canada Council for the Arts and the Department of Canadian Heritage.

THE CANADA COUNCIL | LE CONSEIL DES ARTS
FOR THE ARTS | DU CANADA
SINCE 1957 | DEPUIS 1957

We acknowledge the financial support of the Government of
Canada through the Book Publishing Industry Development
Program for our publishing activities.

Printed in Canada.

99 00 01 02 03 / 5 4 3 2 1

Canadian Cataloguing in Publication data

Lynch, Wayne
Mountain Bears

ISBN: 1-894004-28-0

1. Grizzly bear. 2. Grizzly bear–Pictorial works. 3. Black bear.
4. Black bear–Pictorial works. I. Title
QL737.C27L96 1999   599.784   C98-911208-X

Published in Canada by
Fifth House Ltd.
#9 - 6125 11 St. SE
Calgary, AB, Canada
T2H 2L6

Published in the U.S. by
Fitzhenry & Whiteside
121 Harvard Avenue
Suite 2
Allston, Massachusetts
021134

For Aubrey, as always

CONTENTS

The prominent cheekbones and large muscles of mastication of a grizzly bear give the animal an appealing round facial profile.

A Year in the Life
of a Mountain Bear

I ran as fast as I could, but the young grizzly was faster. As I chased it up a muddy ravine, I realized the fleeing bear was winning the race. With each step that I took through the slippery, gooey muck, my boots and my breathing got a little heavier, and the bear cub got a little farther away. The helicopter pilot, hovering overhead, saw the young grizzly escaping and herded it back towards me. I crouched behind a large rock and waited in ambush. When the little bear bounded past me, I scooped him up with a fisherman's dip net. This was serious bear research, but who would have believed it, seeing me standing there panting, splattered with mud, and wielding a dip net stretched to capacity with my catch of the day—6.5 kilograms (14 lb.) of angry, needle-toothed grizzly cub. Minutes earlier, we had tranquilized the cub's mother and fitted her with a radio-collar to monitor her movements. After we sedated the cub, we laid him beside his mother and left them to recover in peace.

~

I have studied and photographed bears for 16 years, and what has surprised me most is the complexity and richness of their behavior and biology. The more I learn about bears, the more they captivate me. For thousands of years, bears have lurked in the dark recesses of the human imagination and have been woven into a rich fabric of myths, legends, and anecdotes, many of which still exist today. Bear stories are also frequently embellished around campfires, where entertainment ranks above accuracy. In *Mountain Bears* I have tried to focus on the truth about bears, the fascinating biology and enduring beauty of these animals.

Both grizzlies and black bears range well beyond the western mountains of North America, but the focus of this book is mountain bears, the bruins found from the peaks of Alaska and the Yukon south to Yellowstone National Park, and from the Rockies west to the coastal mountains fringing the Pacific shoreline of the continent. Bears are surprisingly adaptable and frequently behave quite differently, depending upon where they live. For example, if you compare a black bear living in the foothills of the Rocky Mountains with one living in the northern hardwood forests of Pennsylvania or in the sawgrass wetlands of the Florida Everglades, you quickly discover that the animals eat different foods, overwinter in a variety of ways, breed at different ages, and differ dramatically in the number of cubs they can raise. By concentrating on the bears of a single region, namely the western mountains, it is easier to understand and appreciate them.

If you are like me, the thought of encountering a bear crosses your mind at some time during every hike, stroll, paddle, or cross-country ski trip into the mountains. On most outings, I'm not lucky enough to see a bear. I may see tracks, a chewed tree, a dropping, or see no signs of a bear at all. However, I always think about these charismatic carnivores as I plod along and try to imagine what's happening in their lives at that particular time of the year. By doing this, every trip to the mountains is a little richer and more rewarding. To help you do the same, what follows is a month-to-month chronicle of the life and times of mountain bears.

JANUARY

ountain grizzlies and black bears may spend six months or more in a winter den every year; that is, half of their lives are spent denning. They do this for the same reason that other mammals den—to conserve energy at a time of the year when food is scarce and weather conditions are severe. Inside a winter den, a bear is lethargic and dormant, a phenomenon called hibernation. Because bears are so much larger than all other hibernators (marmots are the next largest), it is not surprising that the details of how they do it are somewhat different.

In a typical hibernator such as a ground squirrel, the animal's heart beat slows down from 500 beats per minute to a sluggish 25 beats or less, its metabolism drops to 1/25 of its normal level, and its body temperature chills to within freezing. Every 10 to 14 days, the animal wakes up, raises its temperature, and revs its heart rate back up to normal. The squirrel stays active for a day or two, during which time it urinates and defecates, and shortly afterwards it slowly slips back into hibernation for a few more weeks. This pattern of deep sleep interrupted by periodic arousals is repeated throughout the winter.

Bears hibernate quite differently. The body temperature of a hibernating bear dips just 3 to 7°C (5–9°F) below its normal level of 37°C (98.6°F) , and its heart slows to about 10 beats per minute, compared with its normal rate of 50 beats. The biggest difference between a hibernating bear and a hibernating ground squirrel is that, once a bear slips into hibernation, it stays in this energy-conserving state for the entire denning period. Month after month, the bear doesn't eat, drink, urinate, or defecate. This is a remarkable feat of physiology, unique to the hibernating bear. If you or I tried to do the same, we would die in a week. There are records of Alaskan black bears hibernating for 247 consecutive days, or 8.25 months.

FEBRUARY

lk, moose, marmots, red squirrels, and most other mountain wildlife are born in the spring, long after winter has loosened its frigid grip on the land and there is food available for them to eat. Grizzly and black bear cubs, on the other hand, are born in the middle of winter, during the coldest months of the year. At this time, mother bears are hibernating and safely curled inside their winter dens, covered with a thick insulating blanket of snow. The timing of birth is remarkably synchronized within most geographical areas, and commonly all of the female bears living in an area have their cubs within a three- to four-week period, usually extending from the middle of January to the middle of February. Curious biologists wanted to know if a female bear varied the timing of her litters from one birthing season to the next. When they monitored the birthing dates of different female black bears in one area, they were surprised by what they discovered. All the black bear mothers in the study area gave birth to their cubs within 11 days of the dates of their previous litters, and nearly half of them within three days. No one suspected that the reproductive cycle of bears was under such precise control. Grizzly bears have not been studied as closely as black bears in this regard, but it is likely that similar precision exists in the timing of their births as well. The biological cue responsible for synchronizing the timing of birth in bears is the photoperiod, or daylength, and I will talk more about this in the December section.

Newborn bear cubs are homely little critters; they are skinny, wrinkled, pot-bellied, and covered with fine, short hair. Their eyes are sealed shut, and their ears are mere fleshy tabs on the sides of their head. I have often joked that what they lack in looks they make up for in voice, as these little bruins can scream like banshees.

Considering the heft of mother bears, many of whom weigh 90 to 180 kilograms (200–400 lb.), a newborn bear cub is surprisingly small, roughly the size of a chubby adult chipmunk. Young grizzly cubs weigh around 600 grams (21 oz.) and baby black bears are smaller still, weighing just 360 grams (13 oz.). These weights represent about 1/300 to 1/500 the weight of the mother bear. Compare this with the newborn young of most wolves, foxes, coyotes, cougars, and other mountain carnivores, which weigh between 1/25 and 1/70 as much as their mothers, and the average human infant, which weighs around 1/15 as much as its mother. Bears are the only mammals to give birth while the mothers are hibernating, and this is the main reason why newborn bear cubs are as small as they are. During hibernation, mother bears do not urinate, defecate, eat, or drink for many months. In this condition, the mother bear can only withstand the metabolic strain of pregnancy for a short period of time before she must deliver her cubs. After birth, she can sustain the young bears on her milk and still continue to hibernate.

One of the most common questions I am asked about bears is, how many cubs do they have in an average litter? Both grizzlies and black bears commonly have litters of one to three cubs, but rare litters of six have been reported in both species. The age of the mother bear influences the size of her litter, and in general, older females have larger litters. Older bears are more experienced at finding food, and bears in top nutritional condition can nourish larger litters. Even more than the age of the mother, it is the quality of the food supply in her home range that determines how large her litter will be. Where food is scarce and low in quality, such as it is in some mountain areas of the Yukon, the local grizzlies commonly raise just one or two cubs. But in areas like the lush coastal mountains, where food is more plentiful and higher in quality, the grizzlies usually raise more cubs, commonly rearing litters of two and three.

MARCH

In the depth of winter, no one would ever say that the temperature inside a bear den is cozy, but it is certainly much warmer than the temperature of the outside world. In a study of black bears, a biologist determined that the size of an average winter den is just 0.5 cubic meters (18 cu. ft.). Compare that to the average North American bedroom, which is 32 cubic meters (1130 cu. ft.). Using your handy calculator you will quickly determine that about 60 bears could squeeze inside your bedroom, which I think would make an interesting story line for your next nightmare. Since bear dens are relatively small, it is easy for a bear's body heat to raise the temperature inside the den. No one has mustered up the courage to slide a temperature probe into a grizzly den (Where are all those blindly enthusiastic graduate students when you really need them?), but it's been done in black bear dens and the temperatures there commonly hover around the freezing point, even when outside temperatures plummet to frigid subzero levels.

Newborn bear cubs scream loudly whenever they get cold, hungry, or frightened. Their loud voices may be a necessary adaptation for survival, since the mother bear is hibernating when her cubs are born and may be drowsy and slow to react. A cub's loud squeal alerts the mother bear that her offspring needs her attention.

Bear cubs are just as noisy when they are nursing. Both black bear and grizzly cubs produce a continuous loud humming sound anytime they are nursing. Biologists call this characteristic suckling noise the "nursing chuckle," and it is loud enough that I have heard it while standing outside the winter den of a family of black bears. No other baby animal hums in this way. Most researchers

Black bears and grizzlies are found in all of the major mountain habitats, from the aspen groves of valley bottoms, through the spruce and fir forests of subalpine slopes, to the treeless tundra of alpine peaks.

believe the hum evolved in bears so that cubs could signal to their sleepy mother to stay in one position and release her milk. Newborn bear cubs are small and premature at birth and have a lot of growing to do before they leave the family den. Milk is the food that fuels their growth. Both mountain bears produce very rich milk that contains between 20 and 25 percent fat. Compare that to whole cow's milk, which contains just 4 percent fat, and human breast milk, which is even less fatty. The composition of milk in different mammals reflects the biology of the animal and the urgency with which the mother must transfer energy to her offspring. Bear cubs need to grow fast and become large and strong enough to follow their mother when she eventually leaves the family's winter den.

When food enters the front end of a bear cub, you can expect a responding reaction at the rear end. Mother bears commonly eat their cubs' droppings and drink their urine; this keeps the winter den clean. By doing this, she also recovers some of the fluids she loses through nursing. Because a hibernating mother bear never drinks, she is on a tight fluid ration, and every drop counts. Conveniently, bear cubs will not void unless their mother licks them around the anal area. This behavior enables the mother to recover as much water as possible from the young bears. I once cared for an orphan black bear cub and learned about this adaptation first hand. The cub would not urinate unless I wiped its bottom with a warm wet cloth. As much as I like bears, that was about as far as I would go to fulfill my foster parent responsibilities.

APRIL

Most mountain bears vacate their winter dens during a six- to eight-week period, beginning in early April. No single factor controls the timing of den emergence in bears; rather, a number of factors influence the animals' behavior. Important environmental factors include latitude, altitude, snowfall, and photoperiod.

As you might expect, bears that live to the north den longer than their relatives in the south and leave their dens later in the spring. At the same time, bears that den at high elevations generally emerge later than those denning lower down. In both cases, it may be the depth of the snow, rather than the temperature, that influences a bear's departure from its den. Animals burn considerable energy when they trudge through deep snow. After six months of hibernation, a denning bear may have lost up to 40 percent of its body weight, and conserving the last of its fat reserves is an important consideration.

Differences in snowfall levels may affect the timing of den emergence from year to year in the same area. In many cases, heavy spring snowfalls keep the bears curled inside their dens longer than usual. When the reverse happens, however, and the snowpack melts early, the bears may still stay in their dens, supporting the belief that a number of factors ultimately influence the timing of den emergence in bears.

The photoperiod is another environmental factor that may influence when a denning bear emerges in the spring. The photoperiod, or number of hours of daylight, is one of the most important biological synchronizers of animal behavior in arctic and temperate latitudes. In the mountains, the photoperiod coordinates antler growth in moose, deer, and elk, seasonal color changes in ptarmigan and weasels, the timing of migration in songbirds and waterfowl, and the timing of hibernation in marmots and ground squirrels. Since some daylight can penetrate through the snowpack and reach the depths of most bear dens, researchers speculate that the increasing photoperiod functions like an environmental clock, sending a signal to the bear's brain that spring has arrived.

A mix of physiological factors such as the bear's age and sex, its fat reserves, and its reproductive condition also affect the timing of den emergence. In general, adult male bears leave their winter dens first, and adult females with newborn cubs leave last—as much as four to six weeks after the adult males. The other bears, namely subadult males and females, and adult females with yearling and two-year-old cubs, leave sometime in between. The reasons for the different departure times may be related to the differences in energy reserves and energy requirements that exist among adult males, subadults, and females with cubs.

By the time a male bear reaches adulthood, he has a well-established home range on which he has learned to forage efficiently. As a result, he begins the winter denning period with an ample reserve of fat. Because of his ample fat reserves, the adult male can leave his den early in the spring, even if there is no food available. In addition, an adult male bear can be twice the size of an adult female, and his size enables him to range over large areas and capitalize on widely scattered sources of food, such as carrion, which are sometimes available in spring. Finally, it may be advantageous for adult males to leave their dens early to scout their home range and locate potential mates before the spring breeding season begins.

A female bear with cubs has many reasons not to leave her winter den early. In early spring, there is very little food around, and the search for food would drain a mother bear's fat reserves, which are already taxed by her nursing cubs. Moreover, the colder weather conditions that normally prevail in early spring would require the young bear cubs to burn extra calories to maintain their body temperature; naturally these calories would come from nursing, further depleting the mother's fat reserves. Early den emergence would also expose young cubs to a number of risks. Small cubs might have trouble keeping up with their mother, and since they cannot climb to safety or run fast at this age, they could fall prey to predators, in particular other bears, which sometimes try to kill them.

Subadult bears leave their dens after the early-bird adult males but before the tardy females with newborn cubs. Subadults are the teenagers of the bear world, inexperienced and generally less skilled at finding food than adults. They often enter their winter dens with marginal fat reserves, and if they left their dens at the same time as adult males, the added drain of being active in the freezing cold of early spring would quickly use up the dwindling fat reserves needed to survive the lean times that are typical of the early weeks after denning. Even when a subadult finds a good source of food, such as carrion, it is often driven off by the first adult male bear that wanders along. On the other hand, it's unnecessary for a subadult to leave its den as late as mothers with newborn cubs, since it has no offspring to care for and protect in the security of the den.

MAY

In many mountain areas, hundreds and sometimes thousands of elk, moose, deer, bighorn sheep, and mountain goats succumb to the rigors of winter every year. This valuable carrion is an important spring food for many grizzlies and black bears when they first leave their dens. However, hungry bears are not alone and must compete for the prized carrion with an entire cast of mountain scavengers: ravens, magpies, golden and bald eagles, coyotes, and lynx. In many cases, carcasses are picked clean long before a bear discovers them. But among the scavengers, the bear is king, and once a bear claims a carcass, nothing can drive it away, except a larger bear. A bear may spend a week or more feeding on a large carcass. Both grizzlies and black bears may drag a carcass into thick cover, to hide it from other scavengers. A grizzly, unlike a black bear, may also

Bears are the only mammals known to give birth while hibernating.

spend several hours raking dried grass and leaf litter over a carcass to cover it, and then sleep on top of it. A grizzly will also guard and defend a carcass aggressively from other predators, such as wolves, and in particular from other bears. A grizzly may respond to a human trespasser in the same way it responds to one of its own kind, by attacking. A number of maulings have resulted when hikers knowingly or unknowingly came near a carcass that a grizzly was guarding.

Even when a bear is lucky enough to find some carrion, it's usually not enough to sustain it throughout the spring, and the bear must satisfy its hunger with green vegetation—grasses, sedges, horsetails, and wildflowers. In fact, 80 to 90 percent of a mountain bear's spring diet consists of such greenery. This is the time of the year when bears are under the greatest nutritional stress, since they are poorly adapted to digest vegetation. Plant-eating mammals, such as moose and bighorn sheep, have a multi-chambered stomach filled with specialized microorganisms to break down cellulose and a very long digestive tract, averaging 25 times their body length. These two features enable them to digest green vegetation well and extract the maximum nutrition from the food. Bears, on the other hand, have a single-chambered stomach, no cellulose-digesting microorganisms, and a relatively short digestive tract, about six times their body length. Bears can partially overcome this handicap by eating the most digestible parts of plants, such as the new sprouts, flowers, and seeds, and by consuming great quantities of them. One black bear that didn't make it was examined by an Alaskan biologist. The bear's stomach contained nearly five liters of horsetail shoots. Thus a bear may starve with a belly full of greens. Because of a bear's inefficiency at digesting greenery, most mountain bears continue to lose weight throughout May and into June, and sometimes into July.

JUNE

June is the season of sex for grizzlies and black bears. Typically, the home range of an adult male bear overlaps the range of several females. In one study of black bears, for example, at least 15 females lived in the home range of a single adult male, but two or three is more usual. Bears, for the most part, are solitary animals, so the first hurdle they face during the breeding season is to find each other. Males constantly crisscross their home range, checking the resident females to see if any are receptive. Females in heat are also on the move, making circuits of their home range two to three times more often than normal. The increased movements of both sexes improve the likelihood that potential mates will intercept each other.

Female bears are in heat for about three weeks, but they are receptive to mounting only for a relatively short span of time, just three to five days in the middle of their cycle. Once a male finds a receptive female, he follows her doggedly, tumbles and wrestles with her, grooms her head and neck, and nibbles on her ears. Eventually, if the male is an experienced suitor, the female allows him to mount, and copulation soon follows. I have watched grizzlies mate on three different occasions, and the bears were coupled from 23 to 29 minutes, but there are reports of bears mating for as long as an hour. During the several days that the female is most receptive, the pair will mate repeatedly.

Unlike bears, mating in elk, deer, moose, and other mountain ungulates is a quick affair, often lasting less than a minute. In some cases it may be over in just 20 seconds, barely enough time for the partners to blink. If ungulates can achieve conception with such a brief copulation, why do bears stay coupled so long? One biologist joked that bears are such protracted lovers because no one has the courage to tell a slobbering male grizzly to stop. There is, however, another explanation why bears copulate so long. Among mammals, females are either spontaneous ovulators or induced ovulators.

9

When they are born, all black bear cubs have blue-gray eyes that gradually change to dark brown by the time the young bears are six to eight months old.

Humans are an example of spontaneous ovulators; the woman ovulates during her estrous cycle, regardless of whether there is a man around to mate with her. Bears, on the other hand, are induced ovulators; the female only ovulates *after* she has been physically stimulated by a male. Biologists speculate that the trigger for ovulation in bears is simply the mechanical stimulation of the female's vagina and cervix during repeated and protracted mating. If the male is not vigorous enough in his copulatory efforts, he may be unable to induce the female to ovulate. Such a breeding strategy is advantageous to a female bear because it ensures that only a strong healthy male sires her offspring.

Adult male bears are substantially larger than adult females, a trait which biologists call sexual dimorphism. Black bear males, for example, may be one and a half times heavier than their mates, and male grizzlies may be twice as heavy. In mammals, the most common reason why males are larger than females is that they must compete with each other for the opportunity to mate. A big bear packs a big punch, so the bigger the bear, the more males he can dominate, the more females he can breed, and the more offspring he can father. Humans are also sexually dimorphic, and I have often wondered if this trait evolved in us for the same reasons that it did in bears.

When two evenly matched male bears locate a receptive female, they may fight, and the battles can be serious. Most old adult male bears have multiple jagged scars on their head, neck, and shoulders, the sequelae of former battles. They often have broken canine teeth and torn claws, and are missing parts of their ears. I have seen grizzlies with gaping facial lacerations and broken jaws. In the bear world, as everywhere else, sex is a serious and sometimes dangerous affair.

Since bigger body size normally translates into more breeding opportunities, how might a relatively puny male bear compete with his rivals? Not surprisingly, with brains instead of braun. Researchers in the Rockies of Alberta watched a male grizzly herd a female and restrict her movements to a small alpine meadow, where she was unlikely to encounter another male. The attendant male grizzly kept the female in the meadow until she became receptive and then mated with her. I watched the same thing happen in the tundra of Alaska where a male grizzly, not much bigger than his mate, kept her for at least 10 days in a small isolated valley, again an area not likely to be discovered by another male.

All the herding and guarding by a male doesn't guarantee mating exclusivity. A female bear may be as promiscuous as a male. One female black bear was observed mating with at least four different partners, but the record belongs to a female Yellowstone grizzly that mated 10 times with four males in just two hours!

JULY

For many bear cubs, the June mating season has important consequences. This is when the bear family breaks up. Black bear cubs stay with their mother until their second summer when they are about 1.5 years old. Young grizzlies spend an extra year with their mother and leave when they are 2.5 years old, or sometimes 3.5. The bond between a mother bear and her cubs is strongest in the first spring and summer of the cubs' lives. She checks their whereabouts constantly, frets when they are missing, and responds promptly when they whine. The family moves as a unit, its daily movements stalled by periodic bouts of nursing.

In their first autumn, the mother bear allows her cubs more freedom, and the trend continues thereafter. By the time the family breaks up, the young bears have become quite independent little bruins, often spending time away from their mother and foraging as far away as a kilometer (0.6 mi.). Until this point in a cub's life, however, anytime the family encountered an adult male bear the mother moved away, and the cubs learned to fear them. But life is full of surprises for the young bears, and one June, when black bear cubs are 1.5 years old and grizzlies 2.5, their mother no longer flees when males come sniffing around. The presence of these large males frightens the young bears, and many run off, never reuniting with their mother again.

Occasionally, some cubs return to their mother after the breeding season is over. In a black bear study in Idaho, mother bears were sometimes joined by one or both of their yearlings later in the summer. Invariably, however, the families split up in the autumn, and the mother and yearlings denned separately that winter.

When a family of black bears breaks up, the siblings separate from each other at about the same time that they separate from their mother. Afterwards, the young bears wander alone. With grizzlies, the story is sometimes a little different. When grizzly families break up, some of the young bears may stay with their siblings for the rest of the summer, possibly for companionship and security. One trio of grizzly cubs in Jasper National Park, Alberta, stayed together for two years until they were were 4.5 years old. During that time, the young bears even denned together in winter.

The western skunk cabbage is one of the spring foods eaten by mountain bears. The early blooming plant generates its own heat, enough to melt its way through ice and snow.

AUGUST

By late summer, most mountain bears are gaining weight again. Although green vegetation still comprises the bulk of their diets, they eat a variety of other foods that have greater nutritional value. In Alberta, black bears raid wasp nests and tear apart anthills to lap up the agitated insects that well to the surface. In Yellowstone, veteran bear researcher Adolf Murie watched 11 black bears flip over dried bison chips to lick up the beetles and crickets hiding underneath. Murie wrote that "the hillsides were flecked with bison chips of all ages and I was astonished to see that hundreds of these had been tipped over by the bears." Murie carefully recorded that the nutritious insects were only found under bison chips that had aged and dried out. Apparently the bears ignored fresh buffalo pies because they stuck to the ground too much for any insect to hide underneath, not to mention the challenge it would be for a bear to flip a wet chip.

Grizzlies in the mountains of Montana have their own dietary specialties. Researchers were stymied by the big bruins' appearance in late summer on scree slopes of Glacier National Park, at altitudes up to 3350 meters (11,000 ft.). Hadn't the bears read the technical papers? Scree slopes are not good habitat for bears, so why were the animals wasting their time there? It turns out that the bears were feeding on clusters of army cutworm moths. In mid to late summer, the moths fly into the mountains to escape the heat of the prairies. The moths, consisting of 24 percent protein and 34 percent fat, are far more nutritious than any green vegetation. The cunning bears apparently locate the clusters of moths by watching the movements of ravens, rosy finches, and Clark's nutcrackers, which also feed on these nourishing insects. As well, the moths produce volatile ammonia, and the bears may use their sensitive noses to sniff them out.

Berries are one of the most important late summer foods for both black bears and grizzlies. In the mountains, the bruins gobble up blueberries, soapberries, crowberries, and the crimson fruit of mountain ash. A grizzly in the southern Yukon may eat 200,000 soapberries in a single day! What I find even more remarkable than the quantity of fruit a bear eats is the fact that some researcher actually teased apart turd after turd, to count the seeds.

A good berry crop may lure a number of bears to the same area. On a mountain slope of Montana, researchers counted 11 black bears feeding together on the same patch of blueberries. At times, half a dozen grizzlies may graze in the same alpine sedge meadow. For much of their lives, bears are solitary beasts, but when they do come together where food is concentrated and plentiful, they need some way to maintain social order. They do this within a hierarchy or pecking order.

From the time a bear is a young cub, it learns to assess its own rank in the hierarchy and to recognize the ranks of other bears. Generally big bears dominate small bears, and older bears dominate younger bears. Because of this, adult males are at the top of the hierarchy. Females with cubs rank second, and solitary adult females rank third, followed by subadults. Naturally, cubs rank the lowest. A hierarchy helps to minimize fighting and prevent injuries that might result from a fight, and is generally a peaceful way to settle confrontations.

Bears, unlike wolves, foxes, and cougars, don't have much of a tail to use in communication, and their faces are not as expressive either. As a result, grizzlies and black bears rely on body posture —the position of their head (high or low, facing forward or looking away), the position of their ears (erect or flattened), and the position of their mouth (closed or open)—combined with subtle lip movements to communicate their intentions.

Bears also use a number of different vocalizations, including lip smacks, jaw pops, growls, snorts, and bellows. Veteran bear researcher Dr. Stephen Herrero believes that black bears are more vocal than grizzlies because they evolved in forests where visibility was restricted and sound was a more effective way to communicate than visual signals. Grizzlies, on the other hand, evolved in the open tundra where there is good visibility and depend more on visual signals than vocal ones in their communication.

SEPTEMBER

September is the time for bears to really pack on the pounds. Throughout the summer, the animals gradually gain weight, eating between 5000 and 8000 calories a day (most humans eat 2000–3000 calories). But this is nothing compared to what follows in early autumn. The bear's appetite suddenly switches into overdrive, and the bruin embarks on a feeding frenzy, spending as many as 20 hours a day gulping down 15,000 to 20,000 calories, the equivalent of chowing down 43 hamburgers and 12 large orders of French fries in one day. Whoever coined the expression "as hungry as a bear" must have been observing these animals in the autumn.

Gorging bears can really plump up fast. In Yellowstone, one fall, two subadult male grizzlies each gained an average of 1.3 kilograms (3 lb.) a day. In the mountains close to the coast, hungry bears sometimes feed on spawning salmon. When such high-calorie food is available, a grizzly can put on 20 kilograms (44 lb.) in less than two weeks. One bruiser male grizzly, in Alaska, gained 93 kilograms (205 lb.) in 70 days of frenzied feeding. Black bears are no slouches either when it comes to bulking up. There is a report of a male black bear weighing 158 kilograms (348 lb.) in midsummer, and

In spring, when a black bear first leaves its winter den, it may take the animal a week or more to recover from the lethargy of hibernation.

14

when he was weighed again in mid-September, he tipped the scales at 216 kilograms (476 lb.).

The amount of weight a bear will gain in the autumn of course depends upon the quality of its diet. Many mountain bears must work hard to glean calories from greenery, berries, nuts, roots, and occasional carrion. On such a diet, these bears may gain from 0.7 to 1 kilogram (1.5–2 lb.) a day, eventually increasing their body weight by a quarter or more.

Bears are remarkably skilled at finding the most nutritious foods available at any one time. Their survival depends upon it, especially in autumn when they must fatten up in preparation for six months of fasting during hibernation. In September, many plants divert precious nutrients to their roots in readiness for winter, and as a result, roots are a good source of nutrition at this time of the year. Grizzlies seem to know this and commonly dig up the roots of peavine, which contain 30 percent more protein in autumn than they do in the summer.

In the Rockies, calorie-craving black bears relish pine nuts. As the bears climb and claw whitebark pine trees to harvest the cones, their front limbs become coated with pine gum, and when enough dirt and debris sticks to the gum, the whole conglomeration peels off, taking the animal's hair with it. In northwest Montana, in the fall, some black bears can be seen with no hair on their front legs.

Grizzlies also savor whitebark pine nuts, but because the bears are poor climbers, they raid the cone caches of red squirrels instead. A squirrel may stash 2000 to 3000 whitebark pine cones in a pile, at the base of a tree. The brainy bruins break open the cones by stepping on them or biting them, spread out the debris with their nose, and lick up the nuts.

The autumn appetite of a bear seems to be under hormonal control, and if food is plentiful, the bears stop feeding once their fat reserves reach a certain level. In female bears, another factor influences their weight gain: whether they are pregnant or nursing cubs at the time. In one black bear study, the average weight gain of a pregnant female in autumn was 40 kilograms (88 lb.). The following autumn, when the same female was nursing eight-month-old cubs, she gained just 11 kilograms (24 lb.). Keep in mind that in their second winter, black bear cubs stop nursing and hibernate along with their mother, so the energy drain on her is much less than when she is pregnant. The following year, after the family splits up and the cubs have left, the mother bear, who is usually pregnant once more, gains an average of 40 kilograms (88 lb.). The fine tuning of the system is truly remarkable.

OCTOBER

Throughout the mountains, most grizzlies and black bears retire to their winter dens sometime in October. Generally two to four weeks beforehand, the bears move from their autumn range to the area where they will eventually den. Usually they have scouted the location in advance and know where they want to settle. During this time, the bears often appear sluggish and drowsy. It's quite likely that many bears slip into the energy-conserving hibernation mode several weeks before they finally retire to their winter dens. It is important not to confuse hibernation and denning. Hibernation is a lowered metabolic state in which a bear's energy costs are reduced. Denning, on the other hand, occurs simply when a bear rests in one location for an extended period.

In cartoons, bears are frequently pictured living in huge caves, which is not the case in real life. Popular denning sites include the base of uprooted trees, under fallen logs, in the snow-cloaked tangle of brush piles, and even in drainage culverts under roadways. Among the geysers of Yellowstone, enterprising bears may sometimes settle into steam-heated rock cavities and spend the winter in Nature's own sauna. However, throughout the mountains, the most common place for a bear to den is in a simple hole in the ground, called an excavation den, which the bear digs itself.

Excavation dens vary in design. Some consist of a single tunnel, one to two meters (3–6.5 ft) long, ending in an egg-shaped chamber. Others have no entrance tunnel at all, and the chamber opens directly to the outside. Excavation dens are often dug at the base of a tree, or at the base of a clump of alders or willows where the roots support the roof of the den and keep it from collapsing. The one thing that all winter dens have in common is that they are surprisingly small; normally there is just enough room for the bear to squirm around inside. As I mentioned in the March section, a bear can heat a small den more effectively than a large one, and burns fewer calories trying to stay warm, using less of its vital fat reserves.

In many cases, a bear will dig its den over the course of five to seven days, even though it may loiter in the denning area for as long as a month. During that time, the bear eats very little and spends much of its time snoozing in daybeds nearby. Once the den is finished, the animal will sometimes line it with dried vegetation—grasses, leaves, conifer needles, and broken twigs. Generally, the fastidious bruins use their paws to rake the bedding into their dens. I have measured the lining in some black bear dens, and it was as much as 30 centimeters (12 in.) deep. The lining insulates the bear from the frozen ground and may help the animal conserve its energy reserves. In some studies, females with cubs use more bedding than other bears, but this is not a consistent finding.

Many excavation dens collapse after a year or two, so the bears must dig a new one every autumn. A grizzly may move 900 kilograms (a ton) of dirt and rock in digging its den, and the characteristic entrance mound is recognizable from a distance. An experienced bear biologist can sometimes identify an old excavation den 50 years after it has collapsed and been abandoned.

In the Canadian Rockies, both black bears and grizzlies commonly den near the treeline at elevations between 1700 and 1950 meters (5600–6400 ft.), and there is a good reason for this. In winter, when there is a succession of cold clear nights with little wind, temperature inversions develop and the air temperature in valley bottoms may be more than 20 to 30°C (36–54°F) colder than on the mountain slopes near the treeline. Thus, denning at the treeline may earn the bears a thermal advantage, and once again, lessen the drain on their fat reserves and improve their chances of survival.

NOVEMBER

Surprisingly, research about hibernating bears may one day benefit human medicine in a number of ways. Some bone specialists believe that bears may hold a cure for osteoporosis and may prove that bears have "the right stuff" to help astronauts endure lengthy flights in space. In another field of medicine, that of organ transplantation, some surgeons are hopeful that the blood of hibernators, such as bears, may prolong the viability of donor organs, allowing more time for compatible recipients to be found.

Once a bear enters its winter den, it may stay curled inside for six months or more. If you or I were confined to a bed, our bones would begin to thin out and weaken within a few weeks. People commonly believe that, once we stop growing, our bones remain the same throughout our adult lives. Actually, many of the bones in our bodies, especially the vertebrae in our backs and the large bones

*A walking grizzly is pigeon-toed. The animal has considerable rotational movement
in its front limbs, which enables it to dig more effectively for roots and ground squirrels.*

in our legs and arms, are constantly remodelled in response to the workload we impose upon them. If we increase the workload on our skeleton, as with heavy exercise, our body makes these bones stronger. In contrast, if we decrease the workload, our bones decalcify and weaken.

People who are paralyzed or bedridden, or astronauts who are weightless during space flight, put less weight on their bones, and as a result, their bones thin out and become more brittle. This bone-thinning disorder, called osteoporosis, not only affects the bedridden but will also affect all of us at some point in our lives.

As people reach their late forties and early fifties, especially women after menopause, osteoporosis begins to affect them. When bones weaken, the risk of fractures increases. In North America, one-third of all women and one-sixth of men over the age of 65 will fracture a hip.

Orthopedic surgeon Dr. Timothy Floyd wondered whether bears develop osteoporosis when they are inactive in their dens, the way humans do when they are bedridden. Soon he was collaborating with veteran bear researcher Dr. Ralph Nelson. Together they took bone samples from denning black bears and discovered that the bones in these animals had *not* thinned out, even though they had been cramped inside a den without bearing weight for many months. The research continues, but Dr. Floyd believes that "the bears probably produce a regulatory substance which is responsible for maintaining bone mass." If researchers can isolate this bone-preserving substance, it may someday be used to treat and prevent osteoporosis in humans.

Just as exciting is another recent discovery. To begin with, it appears that the same hormone that induces hibernation in bears is also active in other hibernators. This is somewhat surprising, considering that the metabolic characteristics of hibernation in bears are quite different from those of other hibernators, as I described in the March section. It turns out that the hibernation hormone, dubbed HIT (Hibernation Induction Trigger), may somehow prolong the survival time of organs used in heart, lung, and liver transplants. Normally, when an organ is removed from a donor, the tissue deteriorates beyond usefulness within just four to six hours. When the donor organs are perfused with HIT, their survival time increases to 43 hours, a seven- to eightfold increase. At present, 15 to 20 percent of all human donor organs must be discarded because they deteriorate before a suitable recipient can be located. Any method that prolongs organ survival means more successful transplants can be performed, and more lives can be saved.

DECEMBER

In the September section, I described how the size of a female bear's fat reserves controls her appetite and balances her autumn weight gains with her predicted energy needs throughout the winter and early spring. In December, the size of a mother bear's fat reserves also controls the eventual course of her pregnancy. To fully understand how this happens, let's first review some basic reproductive biology.

In a typical mammal, fertilization of the egg occurs within a few hours of mating. The fertilized egg immediately begins to divide until it has grown into a hollow ball of cells, the size of a pinhead, called a blastocyst. Within a week or so of mating, the blastocyst implants on the wall of the female's uterus. From that point on, the growing embryo is fed by its mother through the placenta in the wall of the uterus. After a predetermined number of weeks or months of development, the young mammal is born.

The pattern is much different in bears. After bears mate in June, the egg grows to the blastocyst stage, but then the process halts. For the next five months or so, the pregnancy is put on hold, and the blastocyst simply floats in the cavity of the female's uterus. Then, in late November or early December, the pregnancy suddenly starts up again, the blastocyst implants, and the pregnancy proceeds to completion. This pattern of reproduction is appropriately called delayed implantation.

Female bears benefit from delayed implantation for several reasons. In bears, implantation of the blastocyst occurs *only* if the female has stored enough fat during her fall feeding frenzy to sustain the energy demands of a pregnancy. If the female is too thin, she simply aborts the blastocyst, terminates the pregnancy, and suffers no ill affects. In this way, pregnancy only proceeds when the nutritional condition of the female bear is ideal.

Biologists speculate that bears may benefit from delayed implantation for another reason. If bears were to mate in the fall, breeding activities would seriously disrupt this important feeding period, making it harder for bears to accumulate the fat reserves they need to sustain them through winter hibernation. Delayed implantation is a practical strategy that allows mating to occur early in the summer when feeding is not so critical.

The suspected signal for implantation is a simple and reliable one, the daylength, or photoperiod. In late autumn, the number of hours of daylight gradually decreases. When the photoperiod reaches a critical threshold, it signals the brain of the bear to release hormones that restart the pregnancy and initiate implantation.

Thus, the size of the mother bear's fat reserves determines *whether* she implants or not, while the photoperiod determines *when* implantation should occur. These are remarkable refinements in the reproductive biology of bears. These, and many other topics we have discussed earlier, illustrate how complex and interesting the lives of bears are, and how sensitively attuned these animals are to their environment. Bears deserve to survive. Let's give them a chance to do so.

Most mountain bears leave their winter dens in late April and early May, long before the snow has melted.

Biologists classify bears in the carnivore group of mammals, even though many bears primarily eat berries, roots, wildflowers, grasses, and sedges. Among carnivores, the members of the raccoon and dog families are their closest relatives.

Three yearling grizzlies crowd next to their mother. The young bear on the right is watching another adult female bear that just appeared in the distance.

Nursing sessions for young grizzlies usually last less than 10 minutes, and the cubs nurse every two or three hours. Commonly, each cub in a litter assumes ownership of one or more nipples and always sucks from those nipples.

Typically, yearling grizzly cubs, like the one pictured, stay with their mother for a second year before they finally become independent. Even so, there are numerous records of orphaned cubs of this age surviving on their own.

Normally, in a grizzly family, cubs play with their littermates. Solitary cubs with no playmates of their own age play with their mother, although mother grizzlies vary greatly in their enthusiasm for play.

Normally, neither black bears nor grizzlies are territorial, and they do not defend their home range. Several bears usually share the same neighborhood, and their movements frequently overlap.

When a black bear leaves its winter den in spring, it is still padded with fat. Food is usually scarce at this time of the year, and for a month or two the animal will continue to lose weight.

In Idaho, black bears may kill nearly 50 percent of newborn elk calves. Grizzlies and black bears also prey on mule deer fawns, and moose and caribou calves.

Young black bear cubs have remarkably long,
sharp claws, which the little bruins use to climb
on their mother and crawl through her thick fur.

At the first sign of danger, a mother black bear sends her cubs scrambling up the nearest large tree. Climbing takes practise and strength, and young cubs of this age are sometimes clumsy and slow.

The color of grizzly
cubs varies from tan to
dark brown and may
differ greatly between
littermates.

Grizzly cubs may nurse
for two years or more.
Even so, they often begin
to eat grasses and sedges
as early as four months
of age.

This black bear
excavation den in the
Rockies was located in a
thick stand of lodgepole
pine. From this distance,
I could hear the cubs
nursing inside.

Litters of three cubs are
usually born to older,
well-nourished mother
bears.

After this three-month-old black bear cub climbed up the tree stump, it couldn't get down again and screamed to its mother for help.

On hot summer days, a black bear may dip its front paws in water and rub it on its head, or soak its entire body in a wallow to cool off.

Black Bears versus Grizzlies

	American Black Bear	Grizzly/ Brown Bear
Scientific name	*Ursus americanus*	*Ursus arctos*
Worldwide range	Forests throughout North America 32 U.S. states, 12 Canadian provinces and territories, and 5 Mexican states	Forests and tundra of Europe, Asia, and western North America
Population estimate	450,000 (more than the 7 other species of bears combined)	125,000–150,000 worldwide; 50,000 evenly split between Alaska and western Canada, 800–1000 in lower 48 states
Weight	Average male: 88–154 kg (194–340 lb.) Average female: 60–140 kg (132–309 lb.) Record wild male 364 kg (802 lb.), Manitoba	Average male: 150–380 kg (330–838 lb.) Average female: 100-250 kg (220–550 lb.) Record wild male: 751 kg (1657 lb.), Alaska
Shoulder height	up to 1 m (3.25 ft.)	up to 1.5 m (5 ft.)
Body length	1.5–2 m (5–6.25 ft.)	up to 2.5 m (8 ft.)
Front claws	black, shorter than 4 cm (1.5 in.)	ivory, brown, or black longer than 4 cm. (1.5 in.), up to 12 cm. (4.75 in.)
Coat color	Black or brown western mountains: 10–65% shades of brown	Blond to dark chocolate brown Guard hairs of some bears tipped with white producing a grizzled appearance
Reliable field sign	No shoulder hump	Prominent shoulder hump
Diet	greenery, berries, pine nuts, spawning fish, carrion, climbs to feed on aspen and cottonwood catkins	greenery, berries, pine nuts, spawning fish, carrion, digs up roots of glacier lilies, peavine, wild onions, and spring beauties
Predatory behavior	Both species hunt mule deer fawns, elk and moose calves	Both species hunt mule deer fawns, elk and moose calves
Female sexual maturity	Age 2.5–3.5 years	Age 4.5 years–5.5 years
Average litter size	2–3 cubs	1–2 cubs
Interval between litters	2 years	3 years
Status	Population stable, some local increases	Declining worldwide due to habitat loss and overhunting

The well-developed nipples
on this grizzly identify her
as a mother bear nursing
cubs. Both grizzlies and
black bears have four
nipples on their chest and
two in their groin.

In different regions of
the western mountains,
from 20 to 65 percent of
black bears are colored
some shade of brown.

Aside from its color, the relatively short front claws and absence of a prominent shoulder hump identifies this bear as a black bear.

Even young grizzly cubs a year old may have scars on their muzzle, the result of serious squabbles with their littermates.

A female grizzly may be in heat for several weeks, during which time an attending male will follow her closely, play with her, and groom her, until she eventually becomes receptive to mounting.

*Courting grizzlies may
engage in playful jaw
wrestling, but this varies
greatly among adult bears.
As in humans, some adult
bears are playful and
others are not.*

*Grizzly bears will mate
repeatedly for three to
four days and may stay
coupled for 20 to 30
minutes at a time.*

*A thick stand of cow
parsnip flanks a small
stream in the Columbia
Mountains. The plant is
commonly eaten by bears
and is also a traditional
food of native peoples.*

Rivers throughout the western mountains attract bears. The bruins come to catch spawning suckers, cutthroat and bull trout, and of course, salmon.

At fishing sites, grizzly bears communicate with each other using the position of their head and ears, the gape of their mouth, and vocalizations.

Bears are highly curious and investigative by nature, and this tendency may predispose them to discover novel food sources in their environment.

Grizzlies are strong swimmers, and there are reports of bears swimming as far as 16 kilometers (10 mi.).

URSINE TRIVIA TIDBITS

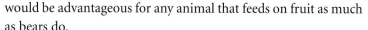orldwide, there are eight species of bears. Half are tropical bears and include the spectacled bear of South America, the sun bear of Southeast Asia, the giant panda of western China, and the sloth bear of India and Sri Lanka. The remaining four are the so-called northern bears, which include the panarctic polar bear, the brown bear or grizzly, the Asiatic black bear, and the American black bear.

◆ The belief that bears have poor vision and are shortsighted has been repeated so often that it is now accepted as common knowledge. There is just one problem: it's wrong. Bears see much better than we think and may see detail almost as well as humans. I have seen grizzlies chase after bald eagles that they spotted over 400 meters (1300 ft.) away. Black bears, and possibly grizzlies, also see colors, and their eyes are sensitive to almost the same range of colors as humans. Seeing color would be advantageous for any animal that feeds on fruit as much as bears do.

During winter, black bears shed the calluses on their foot pads. Sometimes they eat the shed skin, giving rise to the myth that bears nourish themselves during hibernation by sucking on their paws.

◆ Hunting is the main cause of adult mortality in mountain bears. The story is different for bears cubs, which die from starvation, diseases, and predators, mainly other bears. In fact, cub mortality from these causes can be very high. Twenty-five to 50 percent of all grizzly cubs die in their first year of life, as do up to 40 percent of black bear cubs.

◆ One of the most unexpected foods of mountain bears is tree bark. In late spring and early summer, the bears use their teeth to strip the bark from the base of tree trunks, exposing the underlying sapwood. Although the sapwood is 90 percent water, it has a higher sugar content than any other food available at this time of the year. The bears scrape off the spongy sweet sapwood with their front teeth.

◆ All male bears have a bone in their penis, called a baculum. In a large male it is about twice as thick as a ballpoint pen and slightly longer. One of the functions of the baculum may be to mechanically stimulate females and induce them to ovulate.

◆ In midsummer, bears find relief from the heat and pesky mosquitos by returning to the cool depths of their winter den, by soaking in a wallow, or by resting on any unmelted patches of snow. Black bears can also climb high into a tree, to take advantage of a breeze and fewer biting insects.

◆ Some bears are diurnal, some are nocturnal, and others crepuscular, or active at dusk and dawn. The activity pattern of many bears varies throughout the year as their diet changes. However, human disturbance from hunting, logging, mining, farming, ranching, and oil and gas development is one of the most important factors determining the activity cycle of a bear.

◆ From examining a scat, or dropping, a scientist can learn many details about a bear's diet. For example, the spicules on a feather can identify avian prey, and the pattern of scales on a hair can distinguish between a moose, a marmot, and a mouse. Claws, teeth, bones, and beaks are a cinch to identify, as are the seeds of a fruit, the bristles of an earthworm, the antennae of a wasp or ant, and the carapace of a beetle.

Bears are experts at finding the most nutritious food in their home range, including ants and beetle larvae, which they dig out of rotting stumps.

Experienced bear researchers can learn to recognize dozens of individual bears from the differences in their facial appearances.

It is commonly believed that a standing grizzly bear is an aggressive bear about to charge. Most often, however, a bear simply stands on its hind legs to see better so that it can decide what to do next.

When a bear swims, its fur gets wet to the skin. Afterwards, it shakes itself like a dog to get rid of the water.

In summer, bears commonly forage for dandelions and newly sprouted grass along the edge of roadways. Fresh greenery is high in nutrition and easy for bears to digest.

Blueberries and other wild fruit are an important late summer food for all mountain bears. When berry crops fail, hungry bears may be forced to scavenge in camp-grounds and around rural homes to feed themselves.

The front claws of a grizzly can vary greatly in color and length. Those pictured were 12 centimeters (4.75 in.) long and belonged to a tranquilized adult male.

*The sense of smell in a grizzly
is likely as good as it is in a
bloodhound, but there is no
proof for the popular claim
that a bear can detect odors
30 kilometers (18 mi.) away.*

ENEMIES OF BEARS

t comes as a surprise to many people that bears, with their reputation for power, weaponry, and ferocity, have enemies at all, yet bears are sometimes killed and eaten by various carnivores. The most common killers of bears are other bears. The winter denning period is one of the most vulnerable times for a bear. In winter, the animal can be easily surprised and cornered in its den, and it may be unable to flee or defend itself. There are a number of examples of this happening in Alberta, when denning black bears were preyed upon by others of their own kind. Not surprisingly, the attacker is usually a larger, more powerful animal than the victim. In one instance, a large adult male weighing 139 kilograms (306 lb.) attacked a denning subadult male, weighing just 60 kilograms (132 lb.). The predator broke the smaller bear's neck and then ate half of its body. Another time in October, an adult male black bear tore through the ceiling of a female's den, killed her, and fed on her for several days before researchers accidentally frightened the killer away.

Even large adult male black bears are not immune from attack. One time in Alberta, a large male weighing 160 kilograms (353 lb.) attacked a 5-year-old adult male in his den. Luckily, the smaller bear, which weighed 111 kilograms (245 lb.), escaped with wounds on his head, shoulders, and right front leg.

Throughout the mountains, adult grizzlies are generally larger and heavier than the local black bears. Because of this, grizzlies may prey on denning black bears when an opportunity arises. Again in Alberta, a large female grizzly with two yearlings followed the tracks of a smaller black bear and her two cubs through the snow to the black bear family's winter den. The grizzlies killed and ate the two black bear cubs, but the mother bear escaped.

Wolves are another potential predator of denning bears. Although there are no reports of wolves attacking and eating grizzlies in North America, there is a record of a large pack feeding on a grizzly in

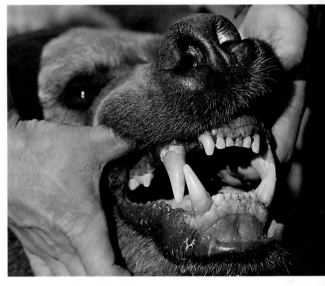

The space behind this tranquilized grizzly's large canines appears empty, but it actually contains tiny, nonfunctioning premolar teeth that a researcher can extract to age the bear.

Finland. The bear's den was nearby, but it was unclear whether the wolves killed the bear or whether they were simply scavenging. There is ample proof, however, that wolves in North America attack denning black bears. In a typical example, a pack of six to nine wolves attacked an adult female black bear and her newborn cubs. All that remained of the family, after the battle, were some scraps of fur, a few fragments of bones, and the cleaned intact skull of the mother bear. Wolf droppings nearby contained claws of the newborn cubs.

A wolf may howl anytime of the day, and in any season. A typical howl lasts about 11 seconds and functions to assemble the pack members and advertise their occupancy of a territory.

An adult wolf is usually smaller than an adult black bear, but what it lacks in size it makes up for in numbers, and there are many accounts of wolf packs attacking and killing black bears.

At the end of summer, young naive ground squirrels are plump in preparation for hibernation. Their inexperience makes them an easy target for grizzlies, and a bear may prey on dozens of them over the course of a month.

During the fall feeding frenzy, a grizzly may pack on more than 1.5 kilograms (3.3 lb.) in a day. Commonly, a bear will increase its weight by 25 to 40 percent, vital fat reserves needed to survive half a year of winter hibernation and the lean times of the following spring.

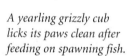

A yearling grizzly cub licks its paws clean after feeding on spawning fish.

Both black bears and grizzlies will readily feed on carrion. Commonly, both species of bears will drag a carcass into thick cover where they are less likely to be discovered by other bears and scavengers, such as ravens and magpies.

During the autumn rut, adult bull elk continually fight and chase rivals. The bulls eat very little during this time, and they lose weight and vigor as the season progresses. Injured or weakened bulls may be preyed upon by large black bears and grizzlies.

Mountain bears may move to their winter dens near the treeline three to four weeks before they actually retire inside. During this time, many bears gradually slip into the energy-saving state of hibernation.

A cinnamon-colored black bear licks ants from the trunk of a tree. Although small, the body of an ant is 50 percent protein and a good source of nutrition.

Soapberries are one of the most important autumn berries for mountain black bears. The bears are clean feeders, ingesting very few leaves and twigs when they pluck the berries.

In late summer and early autumn, ground-hugging plants such as mountain cranberry and bearberry emblazon the tundra.

Some native peoples in the mountains call the bear "the carrier of the medicine" because of their belief in the animal's curative powers.

Following page: In autumn, a grizzly may spend up to 20 hours a day feeding. This bear was stripping blueberries from the stunted plants of a tundra meadow.

*In autumn, a healthy,
well-fed grizzly literally
ripples with fat, which is
usually thickest on the
animal's rump and belly.*

*I took this photograph
from the mouth of an
abandoned grizzly den in
the Rockies of Alberta, at
an altitude of 1950 meters
(6400 ft.). Bears rarely use
the same den two years
in a row.*

Many factors determine when a mountain bear enters its winter den. Cold temperatures, snowfall, and shortening days certainly influence its behavior, but adequate fat reserves are probably the most crucial factor.

The current studies of hibernating bears may someday benefit human medicine. If researchers can determine how a bear stays curled inside its winter den for six months or more and emerges with strong healthy bones, the secret could cure or prevent osteoporosis in humans.

ACKNOWLEDGMENTS

I have studied and photographed bears for over 16 years. During that time, many bear researchers listened patiently to my questions, returned my telephone calls, answered my letters, and invited me into their field camps. More than this, they were always generous in sharing their time, experience, and knowledge. I would especially like to thank Dr. Andy Derocher, Dr. Timothy Floyd, Dr. Dave Garshelis, Dr. Barrie Gilbert, John Hechtel, Dr. Charles Jonkel, Kate Kendall, Wayne McCrory, and Dr. Ralph Nelson. Four scientists deserve special thanks: Dr. Gary Alt, a black bear researcher with the Pennsylvania Game Commission, Alaskan biologist Larry Aumiller of the McNeil River Brown Bear Sanctuary, Peter Clarkson, the former wolf/grizzly biologist for the Northwest Territories, and Dr. Ian Stirling of the Canadian Wildlife Service, one of the foremost bear biologists in the world. These men introduced me to the secret world of bears and helped me to understand them better.

This is my second book with the pleasant and talented folks at Fifth House Publishers, and I again had fun working with publisher Fraser Seely, managing editor Charlene Dobmeier, and designer John Luckhurst. Everything would be perfect if we just had more of those wine and pasta power lunches.

As always, my wife, Aubrey Lang, deserves the greatest thanks. She often camped and hiked with me in bear country and was always a wonderful, stimulating partner. Her zest for life is a constant joy.

ABOUT THE AUTHOR

In 1979, at the age of 31, Dr. Wayne Lynch left a career in emergency medicine to work full-time as a science writer and photographer. Today, he is one of North America's best known and most widely published professional wildlife photographers. His photo credits include hundreds of magazine

covers, thousands of calendar shots, and tens of thousands of images published in over 30 countries. He is also the author and photographer of a dozen highly acclaimed natural history books, including: *Wild Birds Across the Prairies, Penguins of the World, Bears: Monarchs of the Northern Wilderness, A is for Arctic: Natural Wonders of a Polar World,* and *Married to the Wind: A Study of the Prairie Grasslands.* His books have been described as "a magical combination of words and images."

Dr. Lynch has studied wildlife in over 60 countries, and is a Fellow of the internationally recognized Explorers Club, headquartered in New York City. Fellows are those who have actively participated in exploration or have substantially enlarged the scope of human knowledge through scientific achievements and published reports, books, and articles. In 1997, Lynch was elected as a Fellow to the Arctic Institute of North America, in recognition of his contributions to the knowledge of polar and subpolar regions. He is also registered in *Canada's Who's Who.*